THE BOOK OF CLASSIC
BOARD GAMES

Collected by Sid Sackson
and the editors of Klutz Press

KLUTZ PRESS
Palo Alto, California

Illustrations:

Karen Barbour, *Fandango.*

Andrea Baruffi, *Hex* and *Solitaire.*

H.B. Lewis, *Cats and Dogs.*

Elwood H. Smith, front cover, *Checkers, Hoppers,* and *Nine Men's Morris.*

The Southwest Museum, Los Angeles, photographs #CT.387, water jar from Laguna Pueblo, and #CT. 135, Hopi pottery made by Nampeyo, for *Brax.*

Gordon Swenarton, *Dalmatian Pirates and Volga Bulgars.*

Ed Taber, *Hasami Shogi.*

Tapestry for *Brax* woven by Travis Moretti and Christine Laffer at the TAPUS Studio, San Jose, California.

Ken Westphal, *Mancala.*

Chris Wilton, The Image Bank, photograph for *3D Tic Tac Toe.*

Instructive art:

Joan Carol

Book design:

MaryEllen Podgorski

Production:

Elizabeth Buchanan
Betty Lowman

Acknowledgements:

Sid Sackson was our primary games consultant, and Wayne Schmittberger was our primary reader. Both were indispensable. Others who have to be mentioned are Martin Gardner for the original inspiration, Steve Gelb, for his usual contribution of realism, and the Klutzniks, one and all, for the donation of their lunch hours in the name of research.

Additional Copies

For the location of your nearest Klutz retailer, call (415) 857-0888. If they should all be regrettably out of stock, the entire library of Klutz books, as well as a variety of other things we happen to like, are available in our mail order catalogue. See back pages for ordering information.

Klutz

2121 Staunton Court
Palo Alto, CA
94306

Book and pouch manufactured in Korea. Playing pieces manufactured in Mexico and Taiwan.

8 8 8 0 7 5 8

ISBN 0-932592-94-5

LIST OF GAMES

Checkers   page **6**

- Age range: 5 and up ■ Number of players: Two
- Complicated rules? Simple

You can't grow up without learning how to play checkers. One of the world's most popular games. Great for kids and beginners, but room for deep thought exists.

3-D Tic Tac Toe   page **8**

- Age range: 8 and up ■ Number of players: Two
- Complicated rules? Simple

A far, far more challenging game than its two dimensional cousin. Simple in theory, but don't be too quick to move, and don't depend on your luck. It's not that kind of game.

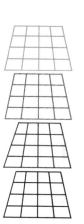

Dalmatian Pirates and the Volga Bulgars   page **10**

- Age range: 6 and up ■ Number of players: Two
- Complicated rules? Simple

A classic siege game. Great for beginners and kids. The Pirates are many, but a bit limited in abilities. The Bulgars are few, but endowed with special powers. A classic from Europe.

Roundabouts   page **12**

- Age range: 8 and up ■ Number of players: Two
- Complicated rules? Medium easy

A game designed for sneaky attackers. Fun and fast. But, as usual, those who slow down and hatch devious plans will usually be rewarded. A classic game originally from Java.

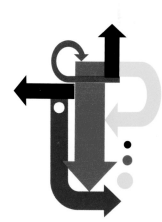

Hasami Shogi   page **14**

- Age range: 8 and up ■ Number of players: Two
- Complicated rules? Simple

If Go is the Asian chess, then Hasami Shogi is its checkers. Probably the most popular board game in Japan. Games usually last 20 minutes.

Go   page **16**

- Age range: 7 and up ■ Number of players: Two
- Complicated rules? Medium

A strategy game for all time. For those who like their plots thick, and their strategies well-conceived, this is the game. Our version is on a 9 line by 9 line "beginners" board, and the scoring is simplified, but it's still the same basic game that masters and novices have pondered over for thousands of years.

Hex   page **20**

- Age range: 5 and up ■ Number of players: Two (or four in teams of two) ■ Complicated rules? Simple

A simple, common sense kind of game that's great for kids and beginners. Quick fun with an edge toward the defense.

Brax   page **22**

- Age range: 7 and up ■ Number of players: Two
- Complicated rules? Easy

A distant relation to checkers. Simple seeming, so it's great for kids and beginners, but there's a depth to this game that will reveal itself to those who care to look—and plan.

Hoppers   page **24**

- Age range: 7 and up ■ Number of players: Two
- Complicated rules? Simple

A distant relation to Chinese Checkers. A great game for kids and beginners. Quick, simple, fun.

Fandango   page **26**

- Age range: 9 and up ■ Number of players: Two
- Complicated rules? Medium

A game with two halves. The first is fast and furious with a high casualty rate. The second is (or ought to be) a good bit more thoughtful. Under its other name, Fanorona, it is the national pastime of Madagascar, an island off of Africa.

Solitaire   page **28**

- Age range: 6 and up ■ Number of players: One
- Complicated rules? Simple

Beginners who play blindly will win this solitaire less than 10% of the time. Experts should win it 100% of the time. The question then becomes, What's your win percentage?

Cats and Dogs   page **30**

- Age range: 8 and up ■ Number of players: Two
- Complicated rules? Simple

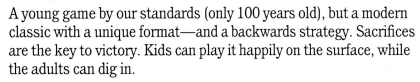

A young game by our standards (only 100 years old), but a modern classic with a unique format—and a backwards strategy. Sacrifices are the key to victory. Kids can play it happily on the surface, while the adults can dig in.

Mancala   page **32**

- Age range: 9 and up ■ Number of players: Two
- Complicated rules? Medium simple

Mancala, and its variations, is one of the five most popular board games in the world today. A classic for thousands of years, Mancala rewards the thoughtful planner every time.

Nine Men's Morris   page **34**

- Age range: 6 and up ■ Number of players: Two
- Complicated rules? Simple

One of the first board games ever invented (1400 B.C.). A quick game that's great for kids and beginners—although luck can be forced out of the game by those willing to go to the effort.

Backgammon   page **36**

- Age range: 10 and up ■ Number of players: Two
- Complicated rules? Trickier than most

Backgammon has a lot of rules, but they're logical. Our version has the world's first set (we believe) to have been written for and by normal human beings. Luck plays just enough of a role to spice it up, but the careful odds player will nevertheless usually win. (Note the "usually.")

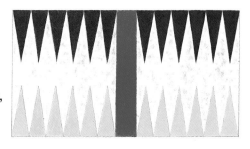

INTRODUCTION

or, "Why we <u>had</u> to find the best 15 board games ever invented."

Suppose for a moment that you and a random sampling of your fellow citizens — all ages, both sexes — have been selected for a history-making scientific expedition. You will all be loaded onto a space-going ark and sent to the planet Xfft in a distant universe. The trip will last thousands of years. Everyone is instructed to bring a toothbrush, enough food (meals will be potluck), and a change of clothes.

A few months before departure date, the recreation director announces that, unfortunately, only a single board game can be taken aboard the entire ark (space is tight). As a result, nominations for the lucky game are being accepted:

"Remember," he says, "the game has to work for all ages. Rules should be straightforward; it has to be multi-

layered so that players of wildly different experience can enjoy it; and there has to be tons of room for strategy for those so inclined. After all, the trip is going to last thousands of years.

Have your submissions in a week before we go."

This was exactly our situation when we began collecting the games that you will find here in this book. The trip, sadly, was called off at the last minute, but not before we narrowed our list of keepers down to a Final Fifteen, all of them certified to meet or exceed the recreation director's criteria.

The first thing we discovered (and it may be as much a surprise to you as it was to us) was how overwhelmingly big our candidate pool was. A staggering number of board games have been created and played over the years. We took a deep breath and started at the beginning.

The first game of which there is any record is "Senet," apparently an enormous fad in ancient Egypt 4,000 years ago. Senet boards have been found carved in numerous tombs and classical references to it abound. We played it. It's a fair game, but when the final cut came, we had to be merciless. In some ways, the years have not been kind to Senet, although it is the root of Backgammon's family tree.

Nine Men's Morris, on the other hand, is a relative newcomer (1400 B.C.) but we liked it a great deal more. It has been played continuously ever since its invention; it combines the recreation director's rare qualities of simple entry (easy rules) with multi-layered appeal; plus, of course, it has 3500 years of successful test marketing behind it. An impressive track record. Nine Men's Morris made the cut.

Right from the start, there were four other games we felt we had to include; these were Checkers, Go, Backgammon, and Mancala. Mancala is played by millions throughout Africa and the Middle East where its variations number in the hundreds; and Go, of course, is virtually the national pastime in Asia. If you add Chess to this list, you almost certainly have the five most popular board games in the world today.

Significantly, if you had compiled a similar Top Five list a hundred years ago, it would probably have read the same. And chances seem reasonable that the Big Five will own the list for another century or so. One can only conclude that there is fundamental chemistry between the rules to these five games and basic, across-the-globe, through-the-ages, human nature.

Not wishing to fight human nature, we put these games in an honored category. They were our only givens.

THE CLASSICS

Mancala

Go   Checkers

Backgammon

Heading toward the Final Fifteen, that left us with ten more slots to fill.

We started by soliciting some expert assistance. Sid Sackson, probably the country's best-known board game authority, spent months culling through his collection of thousands, until he finally came up with a rather lengthy list of candidates which we set about testing in grueling lunch hour sessions.

We tried to be as unscientific as possible, while always bearing in mind the recreation director's instructions (games have to be easy entry, and multi-layered). That took care of an enormous number of games, but as the list started narrowing we installed two more "have-to's."

1. Track Record. All of our games are elderly, with the Egyptian game Nine Men's Morris setting the pace. All of them have had, and in many cases, still have, millions of fans. We insisted on that kind of monster-hit track record because we wanted the reassurance of proven appeal before we installed our last hurdle, our favorite of all. We called it…

2. The Fun Quotient. This was our harshest criteria. After all the games had been played by all of our testers, we pulled together the evaluation sheets. The last blank on each sheet was the biggest, a one-to-ten Applause-o-Meter, or Fun Scale. There were lots of 4's, 5's and 6's. A few 7's and 8's and a handful of 9's and 10's. We closed our eyes and tossed anything less than a 9.

It was at this point that we got the call canceling our trip to Xfft. All of us were secretly relieved. We still had fifteen games and nobody wanted to cut anymore. So as consolation, we took them, illustrated their boards and instructions, and bound them together in the book you're holding in your hands. The best fifteen board games on this planet or any other.

CHECKERS

2 Players

"Checkers" is actually a name given to a family of games, of which there are well over a dozen, all of which use the familiar 64 square chess board. The version given here (called "Draughts" in England), is undoubtedly the most common. It made its first appearance in France, apparently during the 12th century. And yes, Checkers is taken very seriously in the proper circles. Tournaments are held every year both here and in the United Kingdom where champions are able to see as many as 15 or 20 moves ahead.

To Start: Pick 12 pieces of your favorite color. Call them your checkers. Put them on all the black squares of the first three rows on your side of the board. Your opponent, sitting opposite you, should do the same with his/her checkers.

The Play: The object of the game is to capture all of your opponent's pieces, or block them so they cannot be moved. Checkers are always moved

diagonally, one square at a time, towards the other player's side of the board.

Capturing:

You can capture an enemy checker by hopping over it. Capturing, just like moving, is always done on the diagonal. You have to jump from the square directly next to your target

and land on the square just beyond it (diagonally!). Your landing square has to be vacant.

If you have a capture available on a turn, you have to take it. If you have more than one, it's your choice.

Multiple Captures: It is legal, in fact, required, to capture more than one piece on a single move so long as the jumping checker has vacant landing spots available to it that will also serve as legal take-off points for another jump(s).

Kings: If you can get a checker to the last row of the board, that checker becomes a king. Turn it over. Now it can move, or capture, going in either direction—forwards or back, but always on the diagonal.

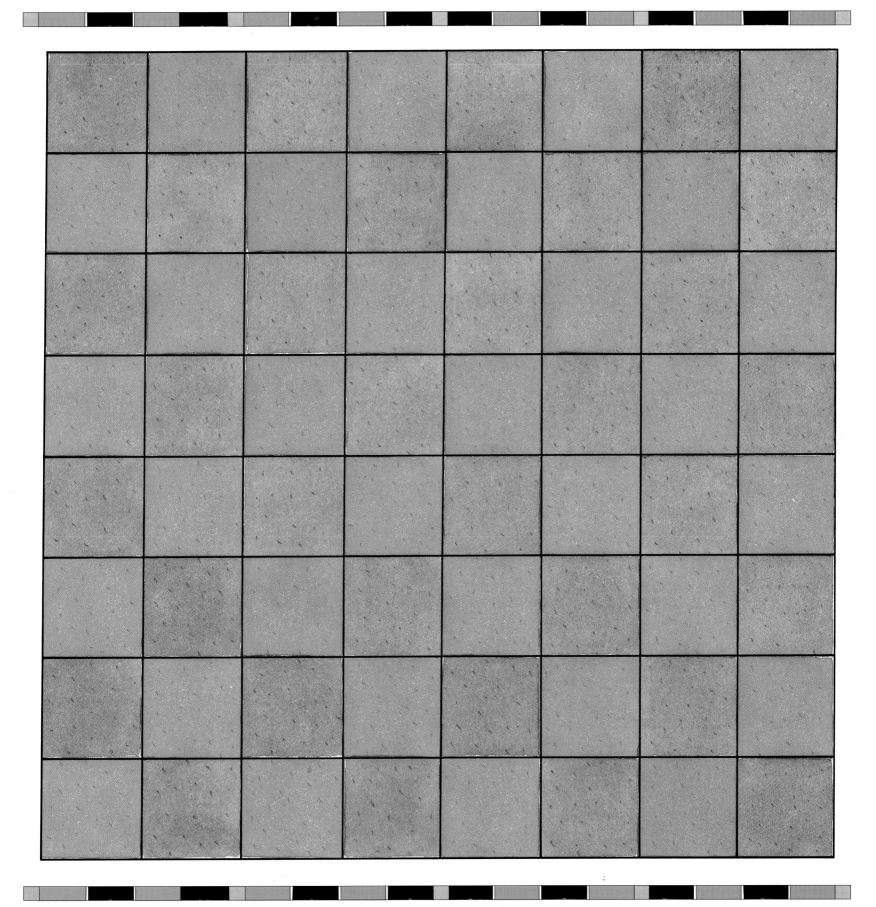

This is a Mach 3 version of two-dimensional Tic Tac Toe, a game that has bored millions over the years. The concept of stringing pieces into a straight line is the same, but the addition of the extra dimension takes the game light-years beyond.

2 Players

The Playing Cube: Four levels, stacked one upon the other, form the cube. A winning line can be made in a number of different ways:

1. A winning line can be straight up and down.

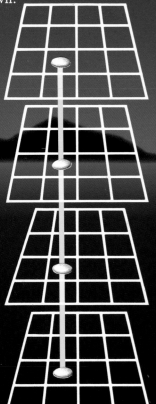

2. Or it can be all on one level.

3. Or it can be drawn on one diagonal, such as from the upper left hand corner on the top level, to the upper right hand corner on the bottom level.

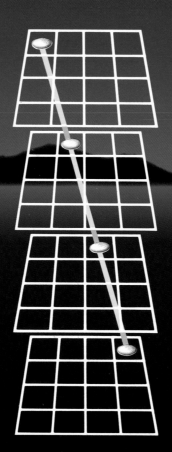

4. Or, a line can be formed across corners. For example, from the upper left hand corner on the top level to the lower right hand corner on the bottom level.

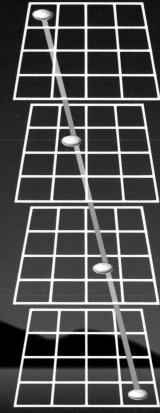

To Start: Each player picks a color.

The Play: Taking turns, each player locates a piece on any empty space.

Winning: Whoever manages to first form a straight line of 4 pieces of their color is the winner.

DALMATIAN PIRATES AND THE VOLGA BULGARS

This is an assault in the classic medieval sense. A well-fortified, heavily armed, badly outnumbered cityfolk (the Volga Bulgars) attempting to hold off an invading swarm of bloodthirsty but exposed raiders (the Dalmatian Pirates).

On the real battlefields of real history, unfortunately, this is a scene that's been played out thousands of times, but it first made it onto the safety of a board game in something called Fox and Geese, and it was a game already hundreds of years old when it became a favorite of the young Queen Victoria in the 1800's.

2 Players

To Start:
Players decide whether they are going to be the townsfolk (the Bulgars), or the raiders (the Pirates). The Pirates are 24 in number, and the Bulgars, an embattled 2. The Pirates locate their pieces on the 24 spaces outside the fortress; the Bulgars locate their 2 on any of the 9 spaces inside the fortress. The Pirates play first.

The Play:
On a turn, players move one piece along a line to an adjacent empty space. The Pirates can only move toward the fortress, (or, I should say, they can't move _away_ from the fortress, since it is legal to go from one point to another if both points are equidistant from the fortress). Once the Pirate is on any of the 9 Fortress points, it can move in any direction it wants either in the Fortress, or elsewhere. The Bulgars can always move in any direction, anywhere on the board.

Capturing:
Capturing is done in any direction by hopping over the captured piece. Only the Bulgars can capture, and only in the following way: the Pirate has to be adjacent to the Bulgar, and the landing spot has to be open.

As in checkers, multiple jumps are possible, although not required, so long as the Pirate pieces are all separated by single open landing spots.

If the Bulgar has the opportunity to jump, he or she must take it. If more than one are available—their choice.

End of Game:
The Pirates can end the game in either of two ways:

1. Occupy all 9 spaces inside the fortress.

2. Trap both Bulgars so that they can't move.

The Bulgars can end it by capturing enough Pirates to make their task impossible.

Winning the Match:
A match consists of two games. Switch sides at the end of the first game to compensate for the fact that the Pirates have a built-in edge. The winner of the match is the player who suffered fewer casualties playing Pirates.

When it's played in Java, where it may well have originated, Roundabouts is called "Surakarta" and is played on "boards" drawn on the ground with shells. In England, though, "Roundabouts" often refers to traffic circles in which English drivers wheel recklessly around a circle and aimlessly enter and exit on any number of "spokes." The result, of course, is blindside mayhem and it suggests very accurately the spirit of this speedy game in which capturing usually comes from unexpected angles.

2 Players

To Start: Let's make you player number one. It so happens you like the color black. So take 12 black pieces and put them on the black dots on your side of the board. Your opponent puts 12 white pieces on the white dots on the other side of the board.

The Play: On every turn, you either move, or capture.

Moving: You can move to any un-occupied adjacent point, in any direction (including diagonally). Remember, moving is done only to *adjacent* points.

A point is the intersection of any two lines.

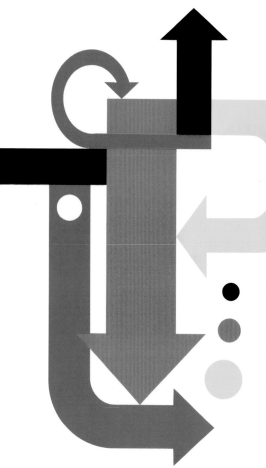

Capturing: Capturing is a lot more exciting than moving because capturing has to be done via a loop, or race-track. There are two racetracks on the board, the inner one (red) and the outer track (yellow). Note that all the points on the board, except the far corners, are on one track or the other, and you can launch yourself from any of them. You can go as far as you like along a racetrack except that you can't pass over another piece, either your own or your opponent's.

To capture an enemy piece, you have to land on its point, bumping it off and putting it in your prisoner pile. However, to get there, you have to travel via a loop or loops. For example, the white piece here could run around the upper left loop to capture the top black piece. Or, it could zoom around all three of the other loops and snag the bottom piece. Important point: you can't run around a loop unless you're going to make a capture.

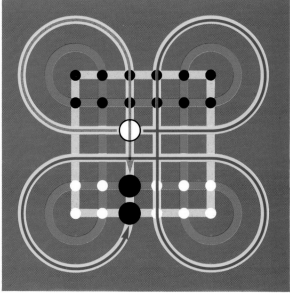

Winning: Let's say you've captured all the enemy pieces. Count the number of your *own* pieces left on the board, and that becomes your score. Play 2 games (alternate who goes first) and add up your scores to find the winner of the entire match.

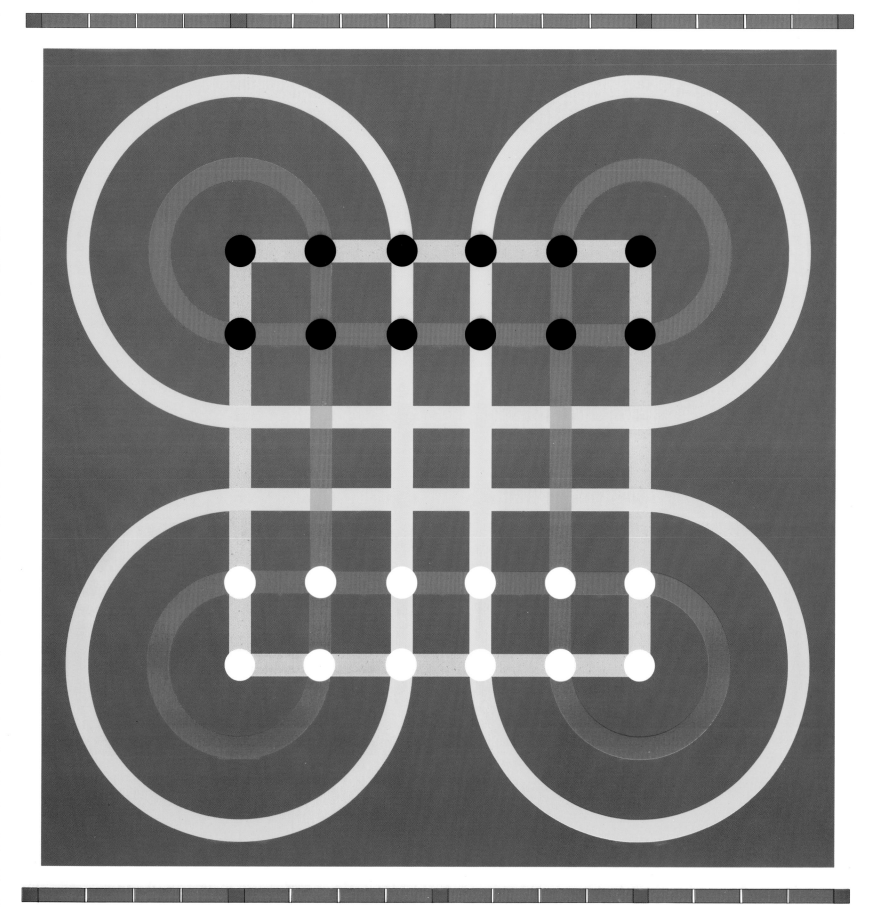

HASAMI SHOGI

Hasami Shogi is a game that co-evolved with the Japanese national pastime, Shogi. It's played on one quarter of a Go board and shares much of the same dignified sense of an Asian land battle. Offensively, the idea is to "sandwich" lines of opposing pieces between two of your own, thereby capturing them. On the defensive side, you have to avoid this grisly fate while building a connected line of five pieces. The rules are a very quick study, but the game peels apart in layers of strategy that provide challenge at every level.

2 Players

To Start: Players pick their favorite color, take 18 pieces of it and put them down on their circles (black pieces on black circles, white pieces on white circles). Figure out who goes first.

Moving: On a turn, a player can move one or more spaces in any direction—forward, backward, left, right—everything except diagonal. All the spaces passed over and the one landed upon must be empty.

Jumping: Players can jump over no more than a single piece, and it has to be adjacent to the jumper's starting spot. The jumped-over piece can belong to either player, and it is not removed afterwards.

A jump.

When a player jumps, he or she must land on the space adjacent (just beyond) to the jumped piece. That space has to be empty, and the jumper has to stop there. Just like moving, jumping can go in any direction except diagonal.

Capturing: Capturing is done by making "capture sandwiches." Here is how it goes. If a player moves or jumps so that their piece becomes adjacent to one or more enemy pieces that are in a straight line (vertical or horizontal, it doesn't matter), and he or she also has another piece at the other end of the line, those in-between enemy piece(s) are captured and removed from the board. Note that there must be no empty spaces in the captured sandwich, which can be any length.

A typical capture sandwich.

Important point: It matters who completes the sandwich. A player may safely move a piece into a line between enemy pieces—forming a sandwich—so long as they build the sandwich, not their opponent.

Winning: A player wins by making a chain of 5 connected pieces of his or her own color in a straight line. The chain can be in any direction—vertical, horizontal, or diagonal. None of the pieces may be in the player's original starting 2 rows.

The War Version

This variation adds a couple of wrinkles. Everything's the same except:

1. The object is to capture all of the enemy pieces, or reduce the enemy to one or no pieces.

2. A piece located in a corner, or a connected line of pieces—of which one is in a corner—can be captured by enemy pieces on both ends of the line. This just means you can make right-angle sandwiches.

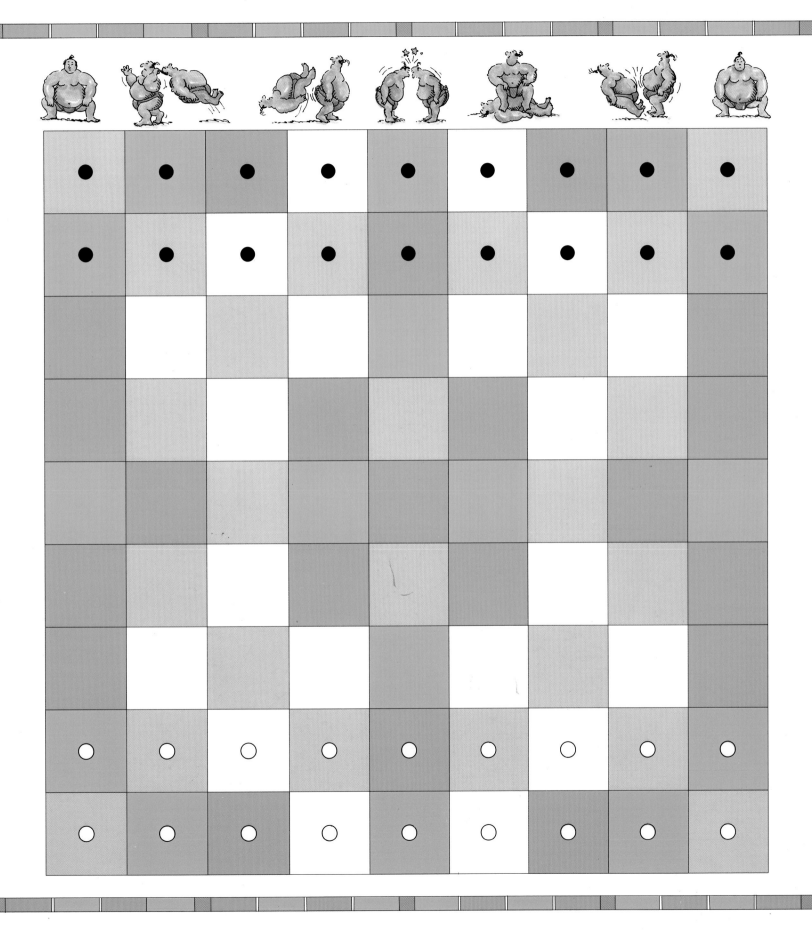

Go

The game of Go has a purity that makes it seem more than human. Its rules are so elegant, and the board is so simple, that it feels more like an act of nature than an invention of man. Indeed the roots of the game are tangled and ancient enough to permit almost any origin theory. The only (nearly) undisputed fact is that it arose in China sometime between three and four thousand years ago, but beyond that, we have only legends to guide us.

Today, the game still enjoys its greatest popularity in Asia, particularly Japan, where it has been played since at least the 7th century. Tournaments with enormous purses are played every year and the games are reprinted in newspapers all over Asia where millions of amateurs hang on every move.

The tournament game of Go is played on a 19 by 19 line board, and it employs a slightly different set of rules from those that are reprinted here, particularly in the scoring. The rules given here are known as "Chinese rules." For the board, we have printed a 9-line-by-9-line "beginner" board. The smaller size has no impact on the rules of the game, only in the complexity of its tactics.

If you become interested in learning "Japanese" rules after you've played by the "Chinese" set, you'll be heartened to know that there are only minor changes in the rules of play. You

won't need to "unlearn" anything. The major differences concern the way the game is scored at the end.

2 Players:

To Start: The board begins empty. Each player starts with an unlimited number of stones. More than enough are provided here.

The Play: A move consists of placing a stone (of your own color) on an empty point (a point is where two lines intersect). Except for some minor restrictions which I'll get to in a minute, play is unrestricted. You can place on any point, including the edges.

Once placed, the stones stay put unless captured. They can't be moved to other points.

You can move or pass on any of your turns, but, in practice, passing only happens near the end of the game. When both players pass in succession, the game is over.

Single Piece Capturing: Go is
a game of "surround and capture." A single stone sitting in the middle of an empty board has 4 open points around it.

"Liberties"

All of them are connected by lines to the stone (i.e., no diagonals). These 4 points are called its "liberties." If all become occupied by enemy forces, that stone is captured. Captured pieces are removed from the board and returned to their owner.

Dia. 1   **Dia. 2**   **Dia. 3**

Capturing on the edge or in the corner is done similarly using the same principle of "no available liberties."

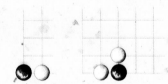

White's turn in both cases. Black is threatened ("atari").

White Captures

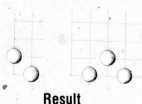

Result

Group Capturing:

Connected groups of stones may also be captured in much the same way as a single stone. That is, if you are able to surround an entire, connected group so that none of its stones have any liberties available, then the entire group is captured and removed. A connected group, here, is defined as stones that "touch each other" with no diagonals permitted.

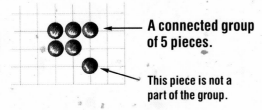

← A connected group of 5 pieces.

← This piece is not a part of the group.

Connected groups live or die as a unit. Individual stones in a group can never be captured individually.

White's move. Black has only one liberty.

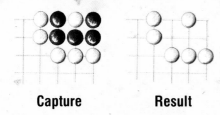

Capture   **Result**

Self-Capturing:

Taking away your own last liberty, or moving to a space that has no liberties, is called "self-capture" and it's occasionally (although rarely) a useful tactic. You remove your suicided pieces in the same move.

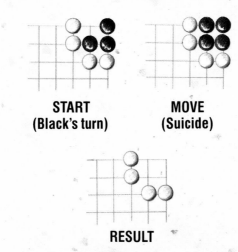

START   **MOVE**
(Black's turn)   **(Suicide)**

RESULT

Simultaneous Surroundings:

If your "suicide" move simultaneously captures enemy piece(s), then it is a capture move, not suicide, and the enemy pieces are removed.

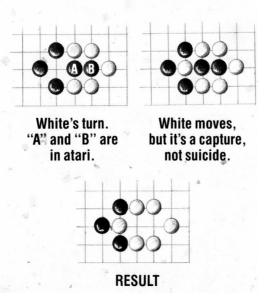

White's turn.   **White moves,**
"A" and "B" are   **but it's a capture,**
in atari.   **not suicide.**

RESULT

No Repeating:

The last rule is simple to say, but it needs an example to make any sense. It goes like this: Board positions may never be repeated. (In other words, if you were to take a photograph of the board at some point in the game, at no time later in the game could the board ever look identical to that photograph.) This is one rule that might prevent your placing a piece on an open point.

Practically speaking, this rule generally translates to mean "no tagbacks." Its primary purpose is usually to prevent endless cycles of capture and re-capture of the same pieces, called "Ko" fights.

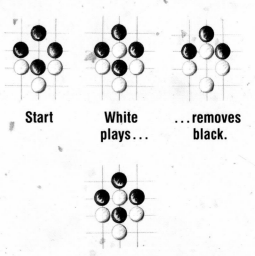

Start   **White**   **...removes**
                      plays...   **black.**

No. Black can't immediately move back to recapture, since that would recreate an earlier board position. If the board later changes elsewhere, then it would be legal.

Scoring:

After both players have passed, the game is over. A player's score is the amount of his "territory," measured by simply adding the number of empty points he has completely surrounded to the number of points he is sitting on. Note that a point has to be completely surrounded by a single player to count as his territory. Points that are not completely surrounded by a player are simply not counted for either.

Winning:

The player with the higher score wins. To keep it fair though, since the first to move has a slight advantage, either play 2 games and alternate the player going first, or add 6½ points to the final tally of the player who moves second. This handicap (called "komi") has been figured specifically for this 9-line-by-9-line board.

Who Won This Game?

Add up all the points that white has surrounded and all the points it occupies. Then do the same for black. Then, since white went second, give it an extra 6.5 points "komi." If you got 44 points for black, and 43.5 points for white, you're a winner—and so is black.

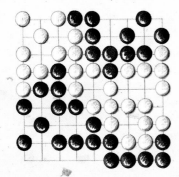

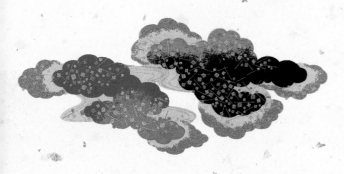

A Small Dose of Go Tactics

Go is one of those games with rules that are so elegantly straightforward that you'll be tempted to skip this part, but don't; it's actually quite important. Without some small understanding of tactics, a couple of Go beginners tend to look like a pair of blindfolded boxers swinging at each other.

The following set of illustrations should help clarify the basics of Go tactics mostly by defining the single most important idea—called "eyes."

A DOOMED SINGLE EYE GROUP

The white group has a single liberty in the corner, and as a result, it is doomed. If black plays on it, he captures the group. If white plays on it, black still "captures" the group since it's a suicide move by white. The single liberty in the corner is called an "eye" of the white group.

A SAFE DOUBLE EYE GROUP

This is a very different situation. The white group has not one, but two eyes. Now, if black plays on one of the eyes, the white group still has a liberty (the other eye), so it is the black piece that is captured (self-captured, actually). This is true no matter which eye black plays on. As a result, this white group is permanently safe. There is nothing black can do to capture it.

ANOTHER DOOMED SINGLE EYE GROUP

Again, a similar looking but actually very different situation. White surrounds two points again, but this time they are connected, not separate. As a result, the white group is doomed. Black can capture it at any time. Prove it to yourself by playing it out. Start with either black or white, and put the pieces on either of the two points in the eye.

A SITUATION UP FOR GRABS

The point highlighted in red is the critical one. If white gets there first, white has a permanently safe group (a "two-eyed" group immune from capture). But if black gets there first, the white group is doomed.

MUTUAL SAFETY

Both groups here are safe, immune from capture by the other player. Why? If either occupies the point marked "X", then it will reduce itself to a doomed single point, single-eye group. It's a stalemate ("seki").

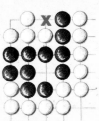

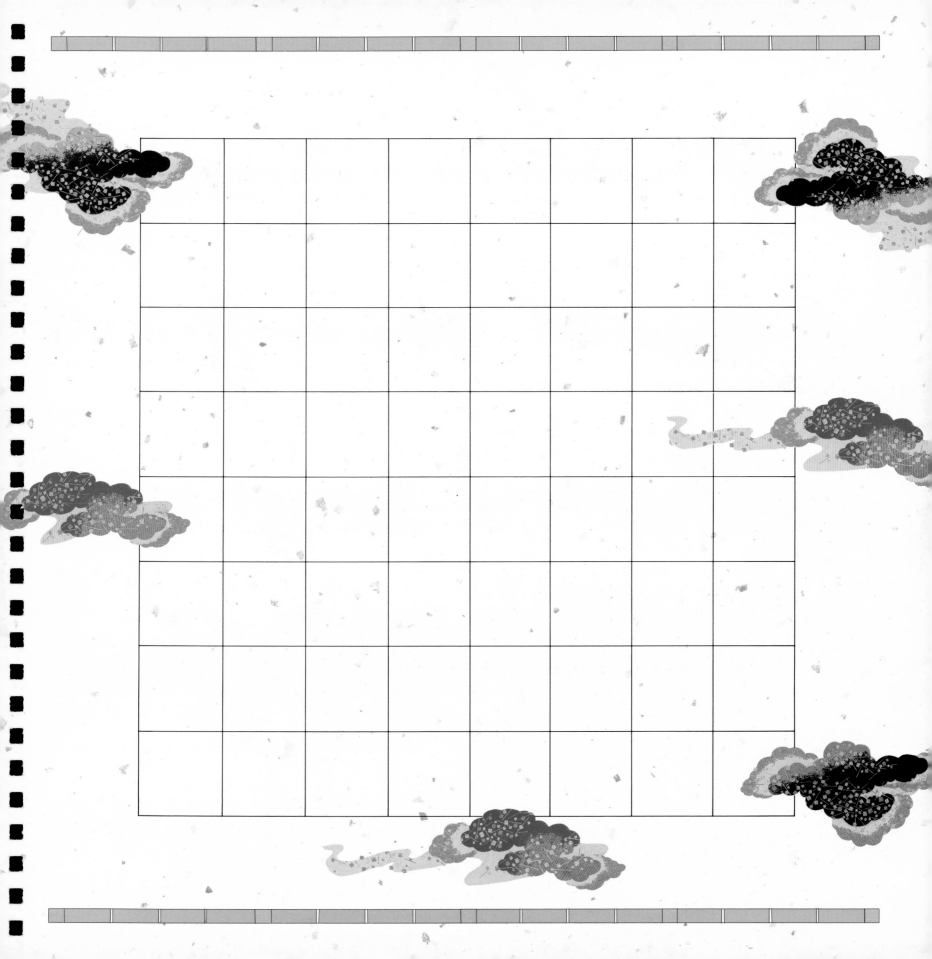

HEX

Hex is a modern game, invented in the 1940's by a Princeton graduate student who concocted the game on the floor of his dormitory bathroom—which was tiled in hexagonals. The idea is to link up a solid chain of your pieces from one end of your board (or bathroom) to the other. The challenge comes in balancing your offensive moves (the ones that get you across the board) against your defensive moves (the ones that keep your opponent from doing the same thing). Relying too much on one strategy or the other will cost you dearly.

Number of Players: 2 (or 4 divided into two teams, with partners sitting across from each other). Play goes to the left.

To Start: With 4 players, turns go around the table to the left. Since the player going first would otherwise have an advantage by starting near the center of the board, start the game like this: toss a coin; the winner puts a piece on the board, after which the loser chooses which color to play.

The Play: The board begins empty. On each turn, players place a single piece in a vacant space. One player (or team) tries to build a chain of their pieces from one black side of the board to the other black side of the board.

The chain can be long and twisty, so long as it has no gaps, and so long as it is all one color.

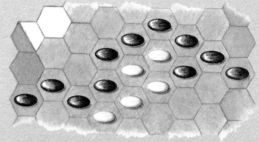

The other player (or team), is trying to go from white side to white side. Corner spaces belong to both colors.

When playing as teams, partners are not supposed to talk to each other.

Winning: First to complete their chain is the winner.

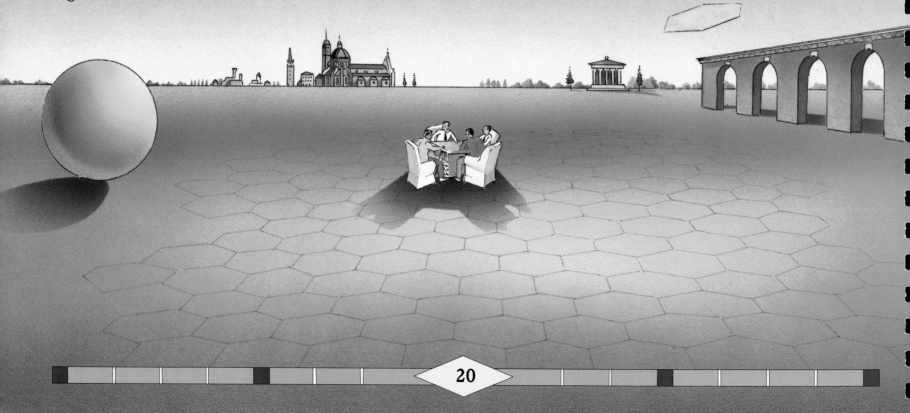

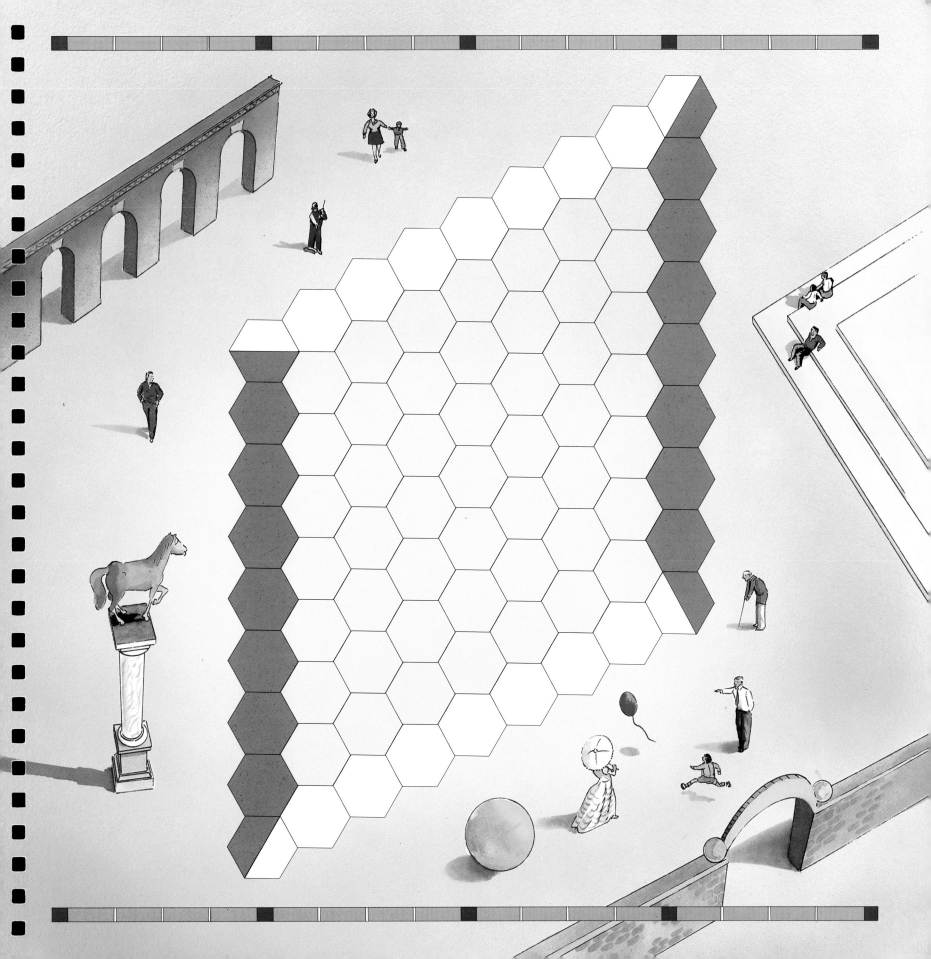

BRAX

Brax is a game nearing its hundredth birthday, and it has lasted because it is a sterling illustration of the Prime Criteria to Good Board Games: i.e., it can be played and puzzled over on a variety of levels. Beginners can blunder through it and enjoy the game for its random action while seasoned players can ponder every move and enjoy its depth and subtlety.

The object is a complete take-over of the enemy forces. Every piece has to be captured. But the quirkiness of Brax has to do with the odd board and the differing way that each piece moves depending on which line it is on. Try it once (it's a very quick study) and then see how deeply you bury yourself in it.

2 Players

To Start: Players pick their favorite color, take 7 pieces, and put them on their diamonds (white pieces on white diamonds, black pieces on red diamonds). Players should take note of the fact that half of the lines on the board are colored white and half are red. White lines belong to the player using white pieces; red lines belong to the opponent.

Moving: As usual, players swap turns. A turn consists of a single move in any direction—forward, back, left, right—on a line. Players can move on their own lines, or on their enemy's lines, but note the following: on an enemy line, a player can move only one point; on a friendly line, a player can move either one *or* two points.

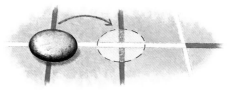

One-point move on enemy line.

Two–point moves can be straight or bent, so long as they stay on friendly lines throughout.

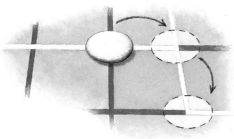

Bent two-point move on friendly line.

A player may not move onto or past a point occupied by a friendly piece.

Capturing: An enemy piece is captured simply by moving onto the same point. It is possible to capture two enemy pieces in a single two-point move on friendly lines.

Braxing: After moving, if a player threatens an enemy piece with capture on the next move, that player may—at their option—call "Brax." "Brax" can be called as long as there is a threat to capture, even if the last piece moved did not create the threat.

On Black's turn, a threatened capture means Black can call "Brax."

Once "Brax" has been called, the other player *has* to move the threatened piece to safety, or, if in position to do so, may capture the threatening piece. If more than one is threatened, they can choose which piece to move.

A player with only one piece remaining may not call "Brax." If their opponent has only two remaining, he or she may not call "Brax" either.

Winning: Simple. Capture all the enemy pieces.

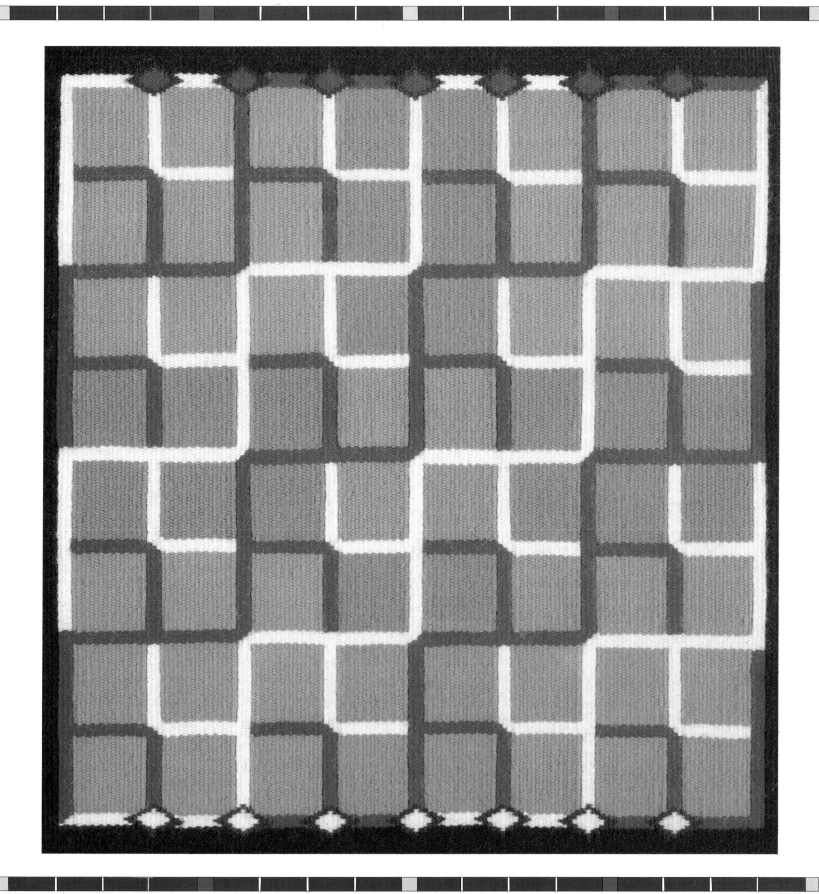

HOPPERS

Hoppers occupies an older branch of the same family tree that gave us Chinese Checkers (which, disappointingly enough, is a modern game invented far from China). The idea is much the same: swarm out from your home camp, battle your way through a no-man's-land, and occupy your opponent's camp—while he does exactly the same in your direction. It's a bloodless battle; no prisoners are taken, but the game goes to whoever can pick and leap his way most quickly through the milling crowd in no-man's-land.

2 Players

To Start: Each player places 15 pieces of his or her color in the spaces of one of the Corner Camps.

The Play: On a turn, a player can either "step" or "hop."

A "step" is moving a piece to an adjacent vacant space in any direction, including diagonally.

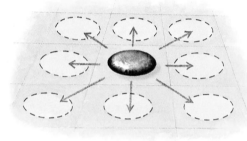

A step.

A "hop" is jumping over an adjacent piece, in any direction, including diagonally, into a vacant space.

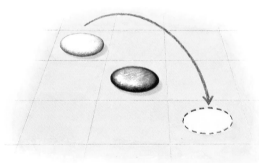

A diagonal hop, not the only legal kind.

If more hops are available for the moving piece, the player can take them or not—their choice. Hopping and stepping are done within the Corner Camp exactly the same as outside it. The pieces hopped over can be either friendly or enemy, and they are not taken from the board.

Winning: The first player to fully occupy the enemy's Corner Camp is the winner.

Note: To stop an obnoxious opponent from simply leaving a piece in their Corner Camp forever so as to block the enemy from fully occupying it, the following rule can be used: A Corner Camp is considered full, even if one or more of the pieces in it belong to the player who started there.

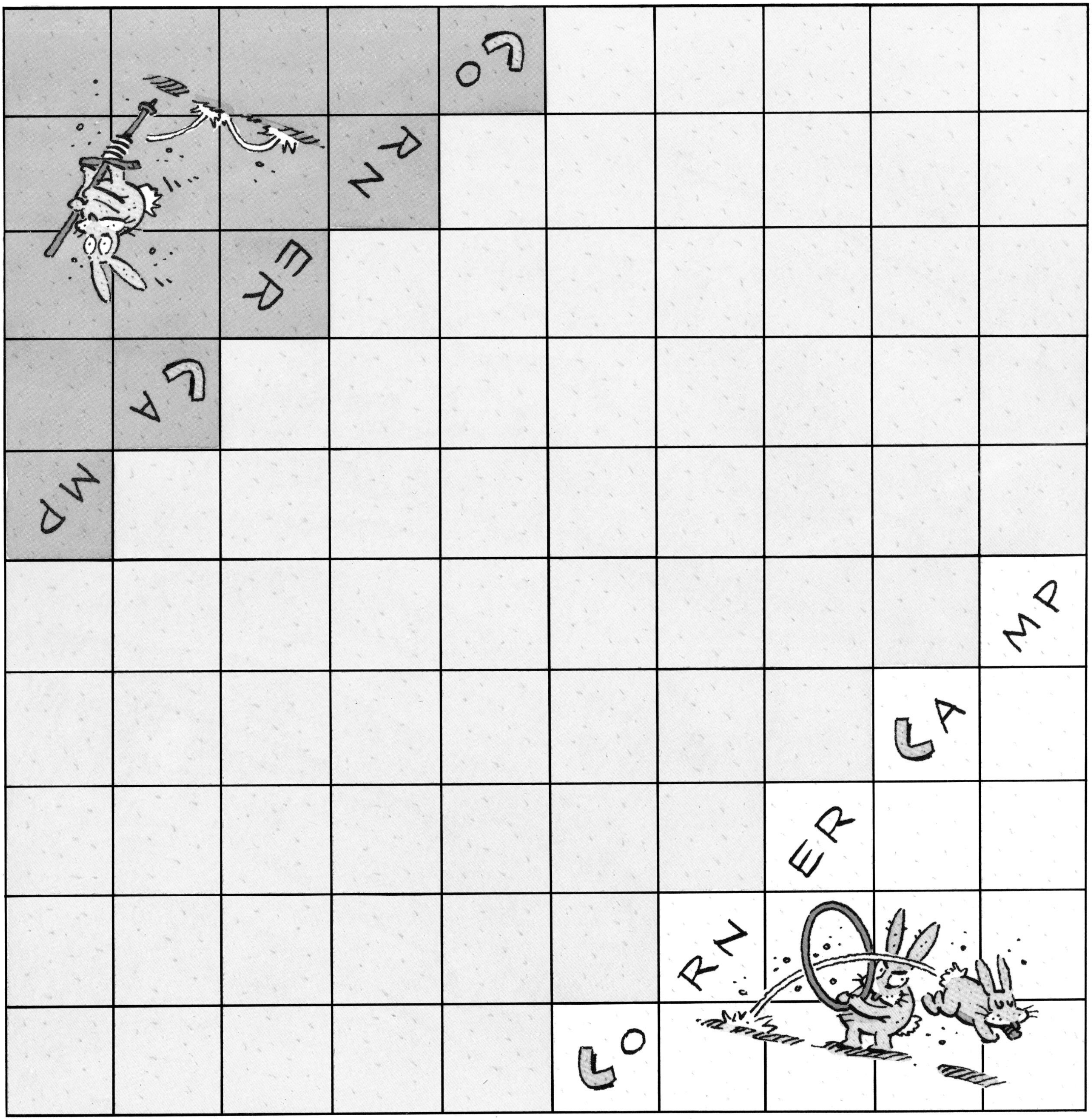
LO
RN
ER
LA
MP

A fast action game that leaves a lot of bodies on the ground in a hurry. Winning is accomplished only by means of a complete wipe-out—you have to capture all 22 of your opponent's pieces. It's a democratic game, all the pieces are equally capable, and capturing can take place either in forward or reverse. As a result, the first half has a very high casualty rate, while the second half gets a good bit more cagey.

2 Players

To Start: Each player puts 22 pieces in the spaces indicated, black pieces on black dots, white pieces on white dots. The central space is left open.

Moving: On a turn, a player moves one space in any direction along any line, into a vacant space.

Capturing: Players can capture in either of two ways, but always along the same line as the movement is made.

1. Approach capture. By moving next to an enemy piece, you can capture that piece—and any others that stretch in a chain away from it along the line of movement.

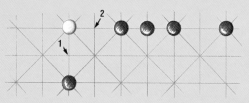

Approach Captures
If White moves to space "1," one black piece is captured. If White moves to space "2," three black pieces are captured.

2. Withdrawal capture. The opposite to an approach capture. By moving *away* from an enemy piece, or a straight line chain of enemy pieces, you can capture those piece(s). Again, all the captures have to be on the "line of movement." Confused? Look at the illustration.

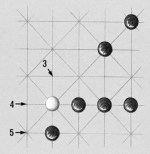

Withdrawal Captures
If White moves to space "3," one black piece is captured. If White moves to space "4," three black pieces are captured. Moving to space "5" would not result in a capture.

If you make a single move that gives you either a withdrawal or an approach capture, you must choose; you can't take them both.

After you've made a capture, you may find yourself in position to make another capture with the same piece. If so, you have to take it. In fact, you can make three, four or more captures on a single turn so long as they are all done with the same piece, <u>and so long as each one occurs along a different line from the previous.</u> (In other words, you must keep moving on a single turn, as long as each move is a capture, and no two successive captures are along the same line.)

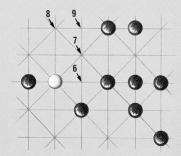

Anatomy of a Single Turn
White moves to space "6" and chooses to capture the single black piece by withdrawal. White cannot go back to the original space. White goes to space "7," capturing one black piece by withdrawal. Then White moves to space "8," still on the same turn, capturing three black pieces, again by withdrawal. Finally, the move to space "9" captures two black pieces by approach. End of turn.

Winning: Simple. Capture all of the enemy pieces.

SOLITAIRE

Solitaire is actually the name of a family of games (there are hundreds of card versions alone). This version of board game solitaire was, according to the story, invented by a French noble-man whiling away his time in solitary confinement. Regardless of the exact origins, the game is a rare find since it satisfies "The Official Two Criteria to a Great Solitaire": One, it is playable in less than 5 minutes; And two, it demands at least as much skill as luck (experts can win nearly 100% of the time, raw beginners, 10%).

One Player

To Start: Take thirty-two pieces. Put them on all the black circles except the one in the center.

The Play: Every move has to be a capture. Captures are made by hopping along a line over an adjacent piece and removing it. You can make a capture, then switch to another piece to make another capture, even if the first piece still has captures available to it.

Continue hopping, and removing pieces, until all available captures have been made.

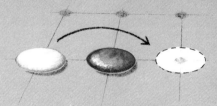

A capture.

Winning: If only one piece remains, that's a second place finish. If, however, that last piece is located on the central point, that's complete victory.

This is checkers from an alternate universe. Or maybe chess with slightly disabled queens. The "queens" in this game are called "Top Dogs" (or "Top Cats") and they can only move with dignity. They are above any bloodshed since they cannot jump or be jumped. The regular cats and dogs, on the other hand, can. The object of the game is to advance your top pieces (be they cats or dogs) to the middle. Clearing their path with well-considered sacrifices is often the road to victory.

2 Players

To Start: First of all, decide which color (and which player) is going to be cats and which color, dogs. Having settled that, each player places 17 pieces of their color on the 17 circles on their end of the board. Flat sides go down.

Each player then takes an 18th piece— with the flat side UP—and places it on their circle marked with a **"T."** (Stands for "Top Dog" and "Top Cat.") Remember, flat side goes up.

The Play: Each player moves one piece in turn. The "top" pieces move one position forward along the <u>heavy</u> line, towards the center spot. If the next position along the heavy line is already occupied, the top piece cannot move until it is empty.

Regular pieces, cats or dogs, move one position in any direction along any line, including the heavy line. Regular pieces, however, may not land on the red dot at the center of the board.

Capturing: Cats and dogs capture each other by jumping, as in checkers. The pieces must be next to each other along a line, and the next position (where the piece has to land) along the straight line must be vacant. Capturing can take place in any direction, along any straight line.

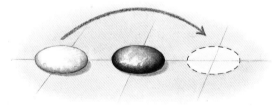

Also as in checkers, multiple jumps can be made if the pieces to be captured are all lined up correctly.

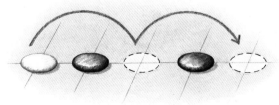

You can change directions in the middle of a multiple jump, just like checkers.

If, in a player's turn, he or she has a piece able to make a capture, that capture has to be made. This goes for single as well as multiple captures. If more than one capture is available to a player, the player is free to choose which one to take.

Top pieces can neither jump, nor be jumped.

Winning the Game: The player who moves their top piece onto the red spot in the center of the board first is the winner. If both top pieces are blocked by opposing pieces and neither player is able to break the impasse, the game is won by the player whose top piece has advanced the farthest along the heavy line.

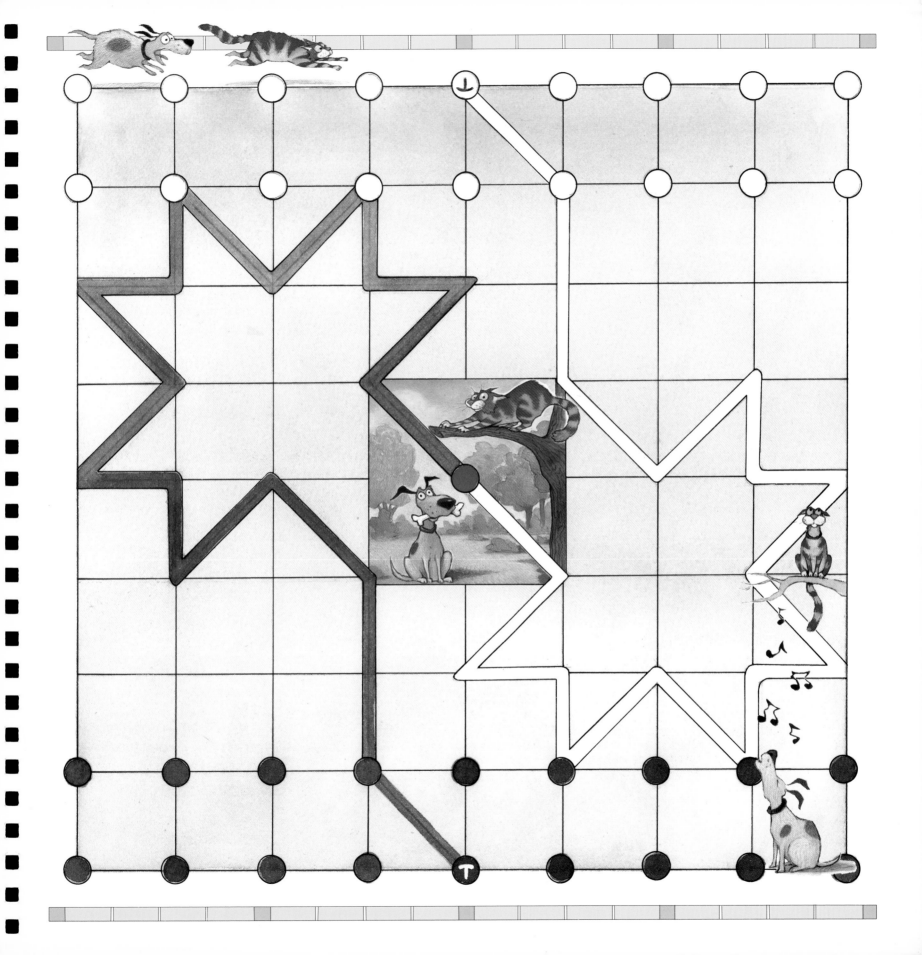

MANCALA

Mancala is actually the name given to a family of games. Our version here is a modernized variant. The games have been played throughout Africa and the Middle East for thousands of years. Our version, like nearly all of them, has a simple surface, but a lifetime's worth of depth to it. Enjoy it on any level you choose.

2 Players

To Start: Each player puts 3 pieces in each of the 6 spaces along his/her side of the board. In Mancala, the color of the pieces doesn't matter. Both players can use the same color, or a mix of colors. It's irrelevant.

The Play: Let's say it's your turn. Pick up all the pieces (or piece, if it's later in the game and there's only one) from any one of the six spaces on your side. Then, moving to the right (counter-clockwise), put one piece in each space you come to (your spaces, or your opponent's spaces; use them both). If you hit your Store, put a single piece in it. If you hit your opponent's Store, skip it.

Free Turn: If your last piece ends up in your own Store, you get a free turn.

Capturing: If your last piece ends up in an *empty* space on your side of the board, you have captured all the pieces in the space directly opposite. Collect them and put them in your Store along with the single piece of yours that made the capture. That ends your turn.

How the Game Ends: When all six of your spaces are empty, the round is over. However, it is usually not in your best interest to be the player with the empty spaces, because your opponent can then place all of the pieces left in *his* six spaces in *his* Store.

Scoring: Count the number of pieces in your Store, that becomes your score. If you're playing a single round, whoever has the most pieces in their Store at the end of the round wins. If you're playing multiple rounds to make a "match," at the end of each round, the player with the most pieces in their Store, counts them and gets a single point for each one over 18. Total up these "over-18" points at the end of a set number of rounds for the match winner.

P.S. If you like, you can substitute an empty egg carton for the printed board here, adding two bowls—one on either end—to be the stores. This might be a good idea if your pieces tend to slide out of their spaces a lot.

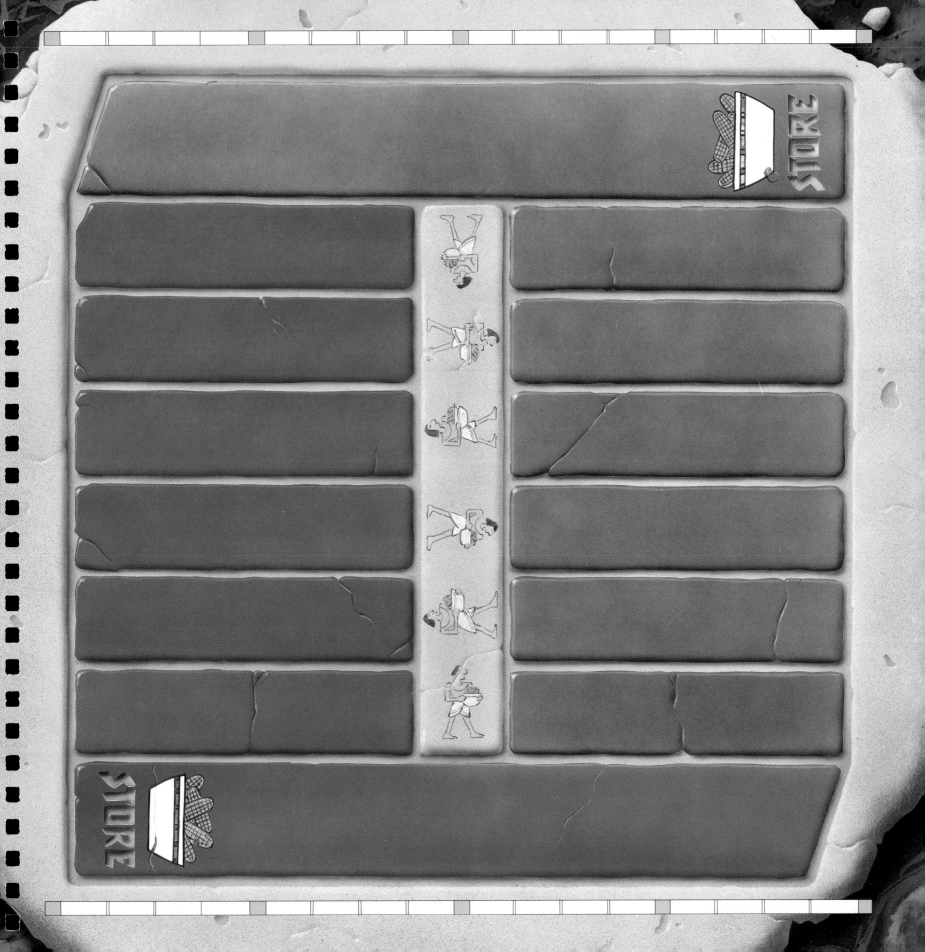

Nine Men's Morris

Nine Men's Morris is now going on its 3,000th year of popularity—give or take. The first board ever discovered was carved by workmen into a temple under construction in ancient Egypt. Later on, the game found its way into the Talmud, King Alfonso's 13th century *Book of Games* and Shakespeare's *A Midsummer Night's Dream*. Over the years, and throughout the world, Nine Men's Morris has been a "fad" countless times. If ever there were an all-time classic game, this would have to be it.

2 Players

To Start: Players start with 9 pieces each, and the board starts empty.

Setting Up: Taking turns, players put all their pieces, one at a time, on 18 vacant points (stars) on the board.

Having accomplished that, players continue taking turns. A turn consists of moving a piece along a line to an adjacent empty point.

Making a String: A string is a complete line-up of 3 pieces—same color—filling all 3 points of a line. Any line counts. Players can make a string either during set-up phase or during play.

A string.

Once a player has managed to build a string, he or she is immediately allowed to grab any enemy piece. The only limitation: an enemy piece from an enemy string may not be removed—unless no other piece is available.

It's legal to break up one of your own strings by moving one of its pieces out and then—if your opponent is napping and doesn't block—putting it back in place on a later move, thereby reforming the same string all over. If you succeed, you can claim another enemy piece.

Winning: A player wins by getting his or her opponent down to 2 pieces. A player also wins if the opponent is blocked so that no move can be made.

Optional Rule: A player who has only 3 pieces remaining is allowed, on a turn, to move any one of his pieces to any vacant space. This is known as "flying" and it's designed to give the underdog a fighting chance.

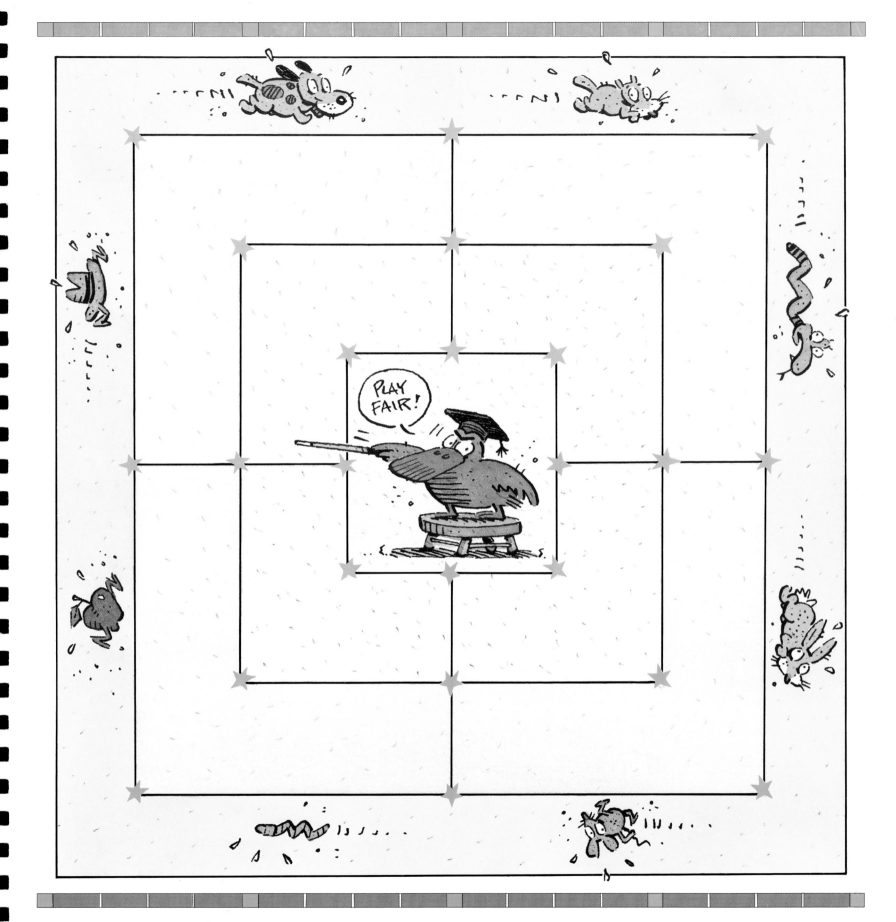

BACKGAMMON

Backgammon is a game that's been on the best seller lists for 2,000 years, earning it the title "One of Mankind's Basic Pastimes." Senet, a game from which it is derived, was found in King Tutankhamon's tomb. But it wasn't until the time of the Romans that Backgammon as we know it appeared.

As you'll no doubt soon notice, the rules are a bit lengthy. But hear me out before you panic and turn back.

Firstly, Backgammon's rules are basically simple, despite appearances. I have been a little windy only in an effort to be excruciatingly clear. You can find much shorter versions on the inside of Backgammon game boxtops, but they lack fool-proof clarity. The basics of the game are logical and there are very few oddball exceptions.

Secondly, Backgammon is worth it. Sixty gazillion fans over 2,000 years can't be wrong.

Thirdly, take it easy on your attention span. Read the first page or so and then start right in. As questions come up, you can refer to the next two pages for answers.

2 Players

Set-up: Set the board up as illustrated at right, and memorize the following vocabulary:
> Your home board
> Their home board
> The Bar
> Points

Now, once you've memorized all that, there's more. You have to remember which direction you and your opponent will always be moving your pieces. The directions are opposite.

The Names on the Board:

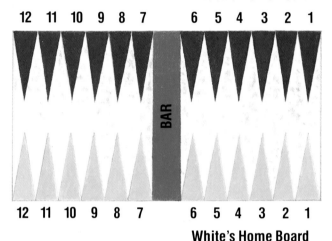

Black sits here.

Black's Home Board

12 11 10 9 8 7   6 5 4 3 2 1

BAR

12 11 10 9 8 7   6 5 4 3 2 1

White's Home Board

White sits here.

How the Game Begins:

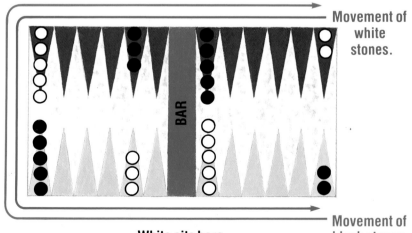

Black sits here.

Movement of white stones.

BAR

White sits here.

Movement of black stones.

The Object: To remove (or "bear off") all your pieces from the board. First to do that is the winner.

To Start: Set the board up as just illustrated. You each have 15 pieces on the board. Get your dice out. Both of you should roll a single die. Higher number goes first. Since Backgammon moves always need the numbers from both dice, the winner here in this getting-started step gets to use the number his opponent rolled as well as his own. How? Keep reading.

The Rules of Play:

1. In Backgammon, players can move any of their pieces at any time. On every turn except the first (which we just covered), a player rolls both dice and uses the two numbers obtained to move his or her pieces. But there are several ways to do this, and the easiest way to illustrate them is by example. Let's say you roll a 5 and a 2. Here's what you can do with that roll.

A. You can move one piece 5 points, touch that point, and then move it again another 2.

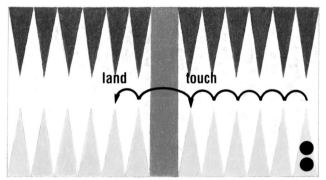

MOVE

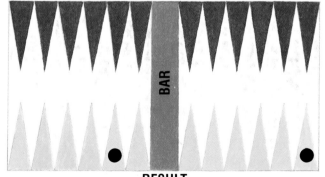

RESULT

B. Or, you can move the same piece 2 points, touch that point, and then move it 5 more. (This may seem the same as A., but it's in reverse order and, as you'll see, that can make a difference.)

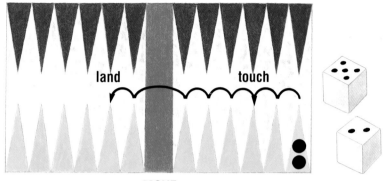

MOVE

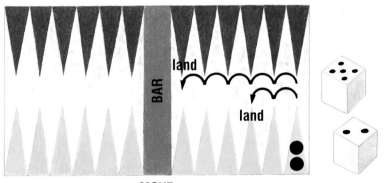

RESULT

C. You can move one piece 5 points, and a second piece, 2 points.

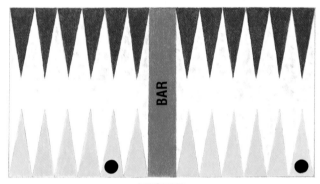

MOVE

Results on next page →

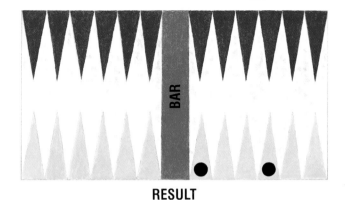

RESULT

2. A double throw is to be wished for (double throws are like a 3 and a 3, or a 5 and a 5, etc.). When you get a double throw, here are your options. Let's say you get a 3 and 3.

You can move your pieces exactly as if you had thrown four dice, all of which came up 3's. In other words, you can move one piece like so: 3–3–3–3. Or, you can move one piece 3–3 and another piece 3–3. Or you can move one piece 3, another piece 3–3, and a third piece 3. Or (are you still there?), you can move one piece 3, and a second piece 3–3–3. And finally, you can move four pieces, each of them 3 points.

As you can see, Backgammon is a game of options.

3. You have to use as many of the numbers you roll as possible. For example, you roll a 4 and a 3. You look at the various ways you can use that roll. As you'll see in a minute, there are times when points are blocked, i.e., you can't land on them. Looking at your options, you realize that among the various ways you can use that roll, only one of them allows you to use both numbers. Other options are closed because they force you to land pieces on blocked points. According to this rule, you <u>have</u> to use the option that enables you to use both numbers. If more than one "both-number" option is open, then it's your choice.

With a double throw, the rule is the same. You have to choose from among the options that let you use the <u>most</u> numbers. And in a double throw, remember, you always have four numbers.

4. On a regular (not double) throw, let's say no option lets you use both numbers, but you do have a couple of single-number options. For example, you roll a 6 and a 2.

Your permitted options happen to be: (a) Move one piece 6, or (b) Move one piece 2. That's all you have. According to this rule you can only choose Option (a) "Move one piece 6." Why? Because 6 is a higher number than 2.

5. If neither of the numbers can be used, the turn ends.

6. By now you must be wondering how to "block" a point. Here is the rule: If a player has two or more of his pieces on a point, that point is "blocked" and his opponent cannot land on it.

7. You may land your piece on any point that is open, occupied only by your own pieces (no limit as to number), or by any point that is occupied by a single enemy piece, called a "blot" (which then becomes "hit" and goes to the bar).

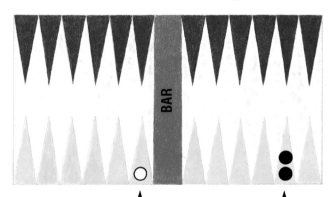

A single piece on a point is "unguarded," called a "blot." | This point is "blocked" by black. White can't "touch" it or land on it.

8. Not only can you not land on a point occupied by two enemy pieces, you cannot even "touch" it in passing. Note the definition of "touching," though. Let's say you roll a 5 and 4, and let's say you want to move a single piece 5 and then 4. But when you move it 5 points, it skips over every point until the fifth where it "touches." That point, though, is blocked by two or more enemy pieces. As a result, you can't do that.

So you go back and look again. You see that if you move it first 4, then 5, the fourth point, the one it touches, is open. So you do it that way. The end result is the same in this instance, your piece moves 9 points, but only one way of doing it is legal.

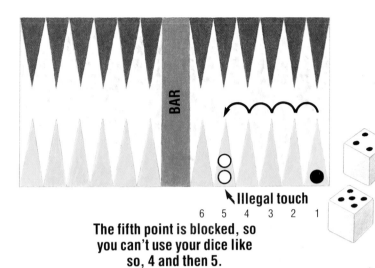

↖Illegal touch

6   5   4   3   2   1

**The fifth point is blocked, so
you can't use your dice like
so, 4 and then 5.**

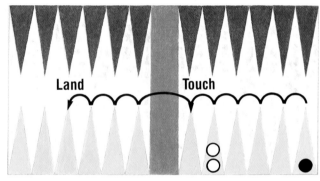

Land   Touch

**You have to use them like so—first 5,
then 4.**

9. If a point is occupied by a single piece, that piece is called a "blot." If you land on your enemy's "blot," or even if you "touch" it and then pass on, you have hit it and your opponent has to move that piece onto the "bar."

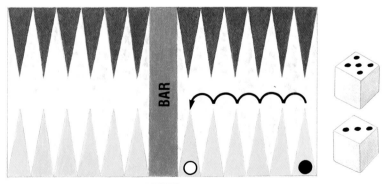

MOVE
Black touches white . . .

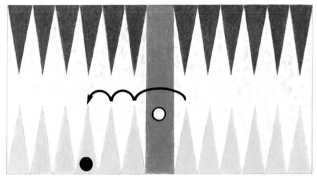

RESULT
. . . sends it to the bar and moves on.

Here's another example of being sent to the bar:

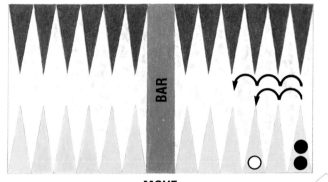

MOVE
Using the 2, black lands on white . . .

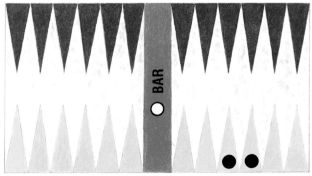

RESULT
. . . and sends him to the bar.

10. If a player has a piece on the bar, then that piece must be re-entered onto the board before that player can move any other piece. Here is how you "re-enter" a piece from the bar.

Let's say you have a piece on the bar as shown in this illustration. You have to get it back <u>on your opponent's home board</u> before you can move any other piece.

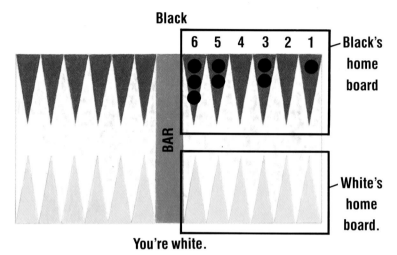

Black

6 5 4 3 2 1 — Black's home board

BAR

White's home board.

You're white.

In this illustration, your opponent's home board only has three open points; the rest are blocked. So (in our example) you need to land on points 1, 2 or 4. In other words, you need to throw a 1, 2 or a 4. (For the purposes of re-entering from the bar, the points are numbered as shown here. Number one is the furthest from the bar, and it's where you'll land if you throw a 1.)

When it's your turn, and you have a piece on the bar, throw both dice (as usual), trying to get your piece back on. If either one of the numbers puts you on an open point in your opponent's home court, take that number. The other one showing has to be used if possible, either by the piece just returned, or by another of your pieces.

When re-entering, incidentally, if you hit one of your opponent's blots, that piece is put on the bar as usual.

Sometimes, your opponent's home board is completely blocked. If that's the case, and if you have a piece on the bar, you can't do a thing until one of his home board points is opened up; so your opponent just keeps taking turns until this happens.

11. You can stop reading now and get started (finally). You won't need this step until somebody gets all 15 of their pieces on their home board. So take a break from instructions reading.

You're back, so somebody must have all their pieces on their home board. Now it's time to win the game by removing (or "bearing off") all 15 pieces. Once a piece is gone, incidentally, it stays gone.

A piece is removed ("borne off") depending on the roll of the dice. For example, if a player has pieces on all of his home board points, and he throws a 5 and a 3, he can remove a single piece from point 5 and a single piece from point 3. Numbering the points, incidentally, the usual way—from out to in.

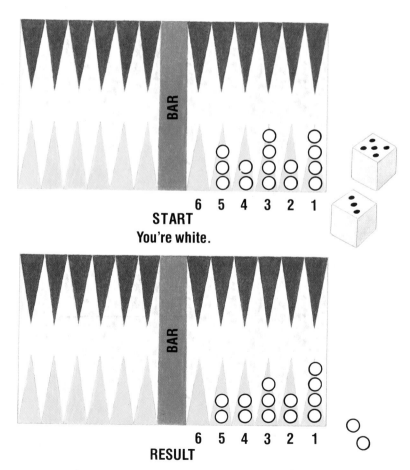

BAR

6 5 4 3 2 1
START
You're white.

BAR

6 5 4 3 2 1
RESULT

Since you always get two (and sometimes, in the case of a double, four) moves with every throw, you can combine "bearing off" with a normal move.

This next point about bearing off is a little tricky, so pay attention.

Oftentimes you will throw a number that doesn't seem to help. You have pieces on points 6, 4 and 1, and you throw a 5 and 3. You are not stuck. Backgammon is a game of options.

The rule goes like this: "If no piece is on the point thrown, the player may still remove a piece from the next point down—unless a higher point is occupied." This is like a horseshoes rule—close is good enough. To follow through on the example started above...

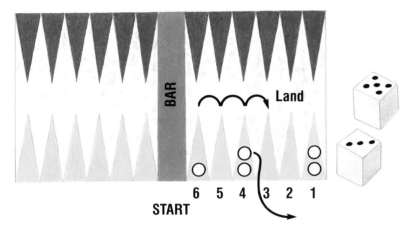

You're bearing off. You've thrown a 5 and a 3. You've got points 6, 4 and 1 occupied as shown. What to do? Use the 3 to move the 6 piece down to the 3 point, . . .

A Last Minute Warning

Let's say you're in the middle of "bearing off," on your way to winning the game, when your opponent attempts to spoil the party. One of your home board pieces is by itself and he hits it, sending it onto the bar. You can't do anything before you get it off, and when you do, it goes back to your opponent's home board. Then, until you get it around to your home board, you can't remove any more pieces. Generally speaking, this whole scenario is to be avoided if possible.

. . . then it's legal to bear off the piece on point 4 with the thrown 5 (under the horseshoes rule).

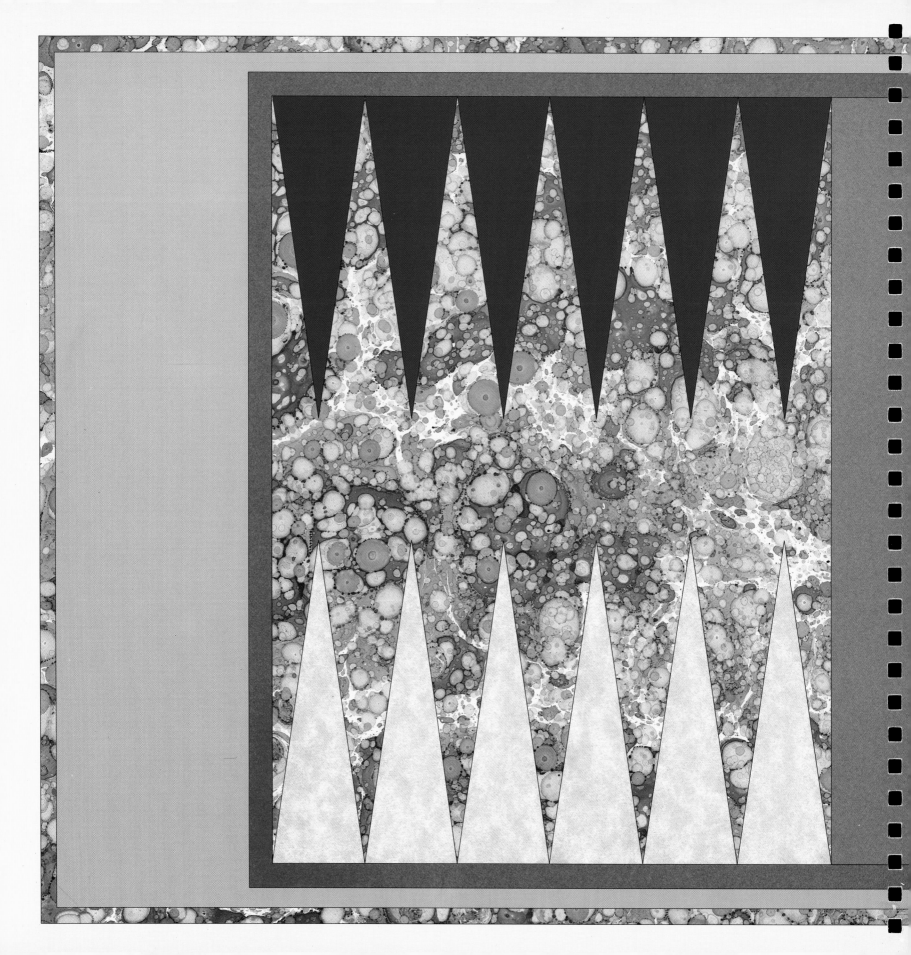

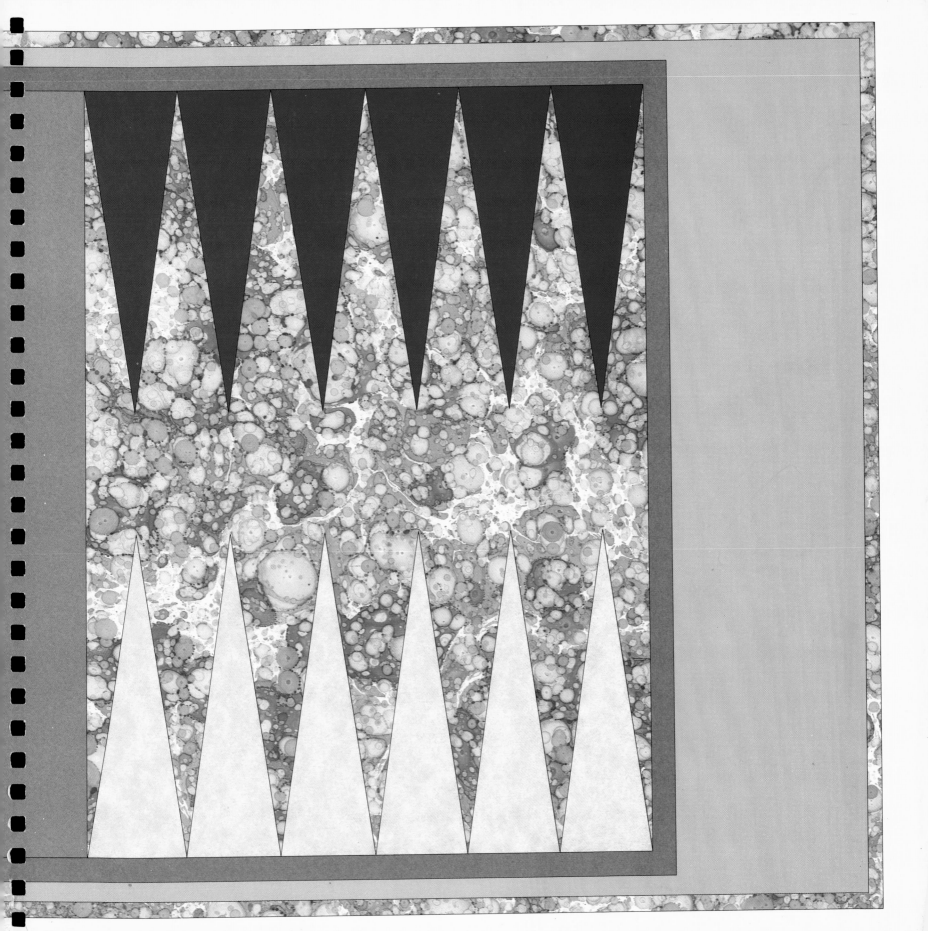

The Klutz
Flying Apparatus
Catalogue

Additional copies of this book, replacement playing pieces, as well as the entire library of Klutz books are all available in our mail order catalogue. It's available free for the asking.

Klutz Flying Apparatus
Catalogue

2121 Staunton Court
Palo Alto, CA 94306
(415) 424-0739